Iulian Bondari

Social Media Organic Growth
From 1 to 1000 Followers

Building a strong social media presence begins with acquiring your first 1000 followers, a milestone that is far more significant than it might initially seem. This book explains the critical role of organic growth in achieving sustainable success. By focusing on organic growth, you ensure that your followers are genuinely interested in your content, leading to higher engagement, trust, and credibility.

This foundation not only boosts your visibility through favorable algorithms but also establishes a loyal community that supports and advocates for your brand. Through practical strategies, real-life examples, and expert insights, this book will guide you on the path to building an influential and lasting online presence.

Whether you are just starting or looking to refine your social media strategy, this book offers valuable tools and knowledge to help you grow organically and achieve your business goals.

Chapter 1: The Critical Role of SEO in Business Success

"SEO isn't just about driving traffic; it's about building a sustainable online presence that attracts, engages, and retains a loyal audience."

Search Engine Optimization (SEO) is a cornerstone of digital marketing, crucial for anyone looking to establish a strong online presence. SEO isn't merely about driving traffic; it's about attracting the right kind of traffic – visitors who are genuinely interested in your content and likely to engage with your brand. SEO helps in making your content easily discoverable by search engines, thereby increasing the chances of reaching your target audience.

The importance of SEO in digital marketing cannot be overstated. It influences organic growth by improving the visibility of your website on search engine results pages (SERPs). A well-executed SEO strategy ensures that your website appears in relevant searches, which can significantly increase organic traffic.

Effective SEO begins with understanding the keywords and phrases your potential customers are using. By optimizing your content for these keywords, you make it easier for search engines to index and rank your pages. This involves both on-page SEO (such as meta tags, keywords, and quality content) and off-page SEO (like backlinks and social signals).

SEO and social media are not isolated strategies. They work synergistically to amplify your online presence. Social media can drive traffic to your website, which, in turn, can improve your search engine rankings. High engagement on social media can lead to more backlinks and social signals, both of which are valuable for SEO.

SEO is a powerful tool that, when used correctly, can help you build a sustainable online presence. It lays the groundwork for organic growth by attracting, engaging, and retaining a loyal audience, ensuring that your digital marketing efforts are not only driving traffic but also fostering long-term engagement and growth.

Chapter 2: Understanding Organic Growth

Why the First 1000 Followers Matter

Your first 1000 followers are critical because they play a pivotal role in establishing and nurturing your brand's online presence. These early followers are not just numbers; they are the foundation upon which your future growth is built. **Here's why these first 1000 followers are so important:**

Authenticate Your Brand

Organic followers are genuinely interested in your content. When your first 1000 followers come naturally, it signifies that your brand resonates with a specific audience.

These followers are likely to be more engaged and more enthusiastic about what you have to offer, providing authentic feedback and becoming early advocates of your brand.

Boost Algorithm Favorability

Social media platforms like Instagram, Facebook, and Twitter prioritize content that receives high engagement.

When you have a core group of followers who interact with your posts through likes, comments, and shares, it signals to the platform's algorithm that your content is valuable. This increased engagement can help boost your visibility on the platform, making it easier for new potential followers to discover your content.

Establish Trust and Credibility

A follower base that grows organically signals trustworthiness. When new users visit your profile and see an engaged community, it lends credibility to your brand. They see that people are genuinely interested in what you're sharing, which can encourage them to follow you as well.

Trust and credibility are crucial in the digital age, where consumers are bombarded with countless options and must decide quickly which brands to engage with.

The journey to your first 1000 followers is not just about reaching a number; it's about building a strong, authentic foundation. This foundation supports future growth and helps ensure that your social media presence is sustainable in the long term.

Chapter 3: Crafting Quality Content

Quality Content is King

Creating quality content is the cornerstone of building a strong social media presence. It not only attracts organic followers but also keeps them engaged and invested in your brand. High-quality content reflects your brand's values, resonates with your audience, and stands out in a crowded digital landscape. **Here are the key elements to focus on:**

1. Identify Your Audience: Understanding your audience is the first step in crafting content that resonates. This involves conducting thorough research to identify their demographics, interests, needs, and preferences. Use tools like social media analytics, surveys, and direct interactions to gather insights about your audience. Knowing who your audience is will help you create content that is relevant and appealing to them.

Consider the following strategies for identifying your audience:

Social Media Analytics: Platforms like Facebook, Instagram, and Twitter offer insights into the demographics and behavior of your followers.

Analyze this data to understand who is engaging with your content.

Surveys and Feedback: Conduct surveys or ask for feedback directly from your audience. This can provide valuable information about their preferences and expectations.

Market Research: Study industry reports and market trends to gain a broader understanding of your target audience. This can help you identify new opportunities and areas of interest.

2. Create Valuable Content: Once you understand your audience, focus on creating content that provides value to them. Valuable content is informative, entertaining, and relevant to your audience's interests and needs. It can take various forms, such as blog posts, videos, infographics, podcasts, and more. The key is to consistently deliver high-quality content that resonates with your audience.

Here are some tips for creating valuable content:

Educational Content: Share knowledge and insights that can help your audience solve problems or learn something new. This could include how-to guides, tutorials, and industry news.

Entertaining Content: Engage your audience with entertaining content that aligns with your brand's voice and values. This could include behind-the-scenes videos, humorous posts, or engaging stories.

Inspirational Content: Inspire your audience with motivational quotes, success stories, and aspirational content. This can help build a positive association with your brand.

Interactive Content: Encourage interaction by creating content that invites comments, shares, and participation. This could include polls, quizzes, and challenges.

3. Visual Appeal: In the digital age, visual content is more important than ever. High-quality images, videos, and graphics can capture attention, convey messages quickly, and enhance the overall appeal of your content.

Investing in professional graphic design and visual content can significantly improve your engagement rates.

Consider the following aspects of visual appeal:

High-Quality Images and Videos: Use high-resolution images and professional-quality videos to create a polished and visually appealing look.

Consistent Branding: Maintain a consistent visual style that reflects your brand's identity. This includes using a consistent color palette, typography, and design elements.

Graphic Design: Utilize graphic design to enhance your posts' visual appeal. Infographics, custom illustrations, and branded graphics can make your content stand out.

Attention to Detail: Pay attention to the details of your visual content, such as composition, lighting, and editing. Small details can make a big difference in the overall quality of your content.

Crafting Quality Content for Different Platforms:

Different social media platforms have unique characteristics and audience behaviors. Tailoring your content to suit each platform can help you maximize your reach and engagement. **Here are some tips for creating content for different platforms:**

Facebook: Focus on creating a mix of content types, including text posts, images, videos, and live streams. Facebook's algorithm favors content that sparks conversations, so encourage comments and shares.

Instagram: Emphasize visual content, including high-quality photos, videos, and stories. Use Instagram's features like IGTV and Reels to create engaging and dynamic content.

Twitter: Keep your content concise and to the point. Use images, GIFs, and short videos to enhance your tweets. Engage with your audience through replies, retweets, and hashtags.

LinkedIn: Create professional and informative content that provides value to your industry peers and potential clients. Share articles, case studies, and industry insights to establish your expertise.

YouTube: Focus on creating high-quality video content that educates, entertains, or inspires your audience. Optimize your videos with relevant keywords and engage with your audience through comments and community posts.

Measuring the Success of Your Content:

To ensure that your content is effective, it's important to regularly measure its performance and make adjustments as needed. Use social media analytics tools to track key metrics, such as engagement rates, reach, and conversions. Analyze this data to understand what types of content resonate with your audience and refine your content strategy accordingly.

Key metrics to track include:

Engagement Rate: The percentage of your audience that interacts with your content. High engagement rates indicate that your content is resonating with your audience.

Reach: The number of unique users who see your content. Increasing your reach can help you attract new followers and expand your audience.

Conversions: The number of users who take a desired action, such as signing up for a newsletter or making a purchase. Conversions are a key indicator of the effectiveness of your content in driving business goals.

Feedback: Pay attention to the comments and feedback from your audience. This can provide valuable insights into their preferences and help you improve your content.

Crafting quality content is a vital component of building a strong social media presence. By identifying your audience, creating valuable content, and enhancing your posts with visual appeal, you can attract and retain organic followers who are genuinely interested in your brand. This approach not only boosts engagement and algorithm favorability but also establishes trust and credibility with your audience. Through consistent efforts and a focus on quality, you can lay the foundation for sustainable success in the digital landscape.

Chapter 4: Engaging Your Audience

Building a Loyal Community

Engaging your audience is crucial for building a loyal community that supports and advocates for your brand. Active engagement helps foster relationships, encourages interaction, and increases the overall visibility of your content. **Here are key strategies to effectively engage your audience:**

1. Active Engagement:

Responding to comments and messages promptly is essential for showing your audience that you value their input and participation. Timely responses can turn casual followers into loyal fans, creating a sense of community and connection.

Consider the following practices for active engagement:

Personalized Responses: Address your followers by name and provide thoughtful replies to their comments and messages. This personal touch can make them feel appreciated and more connected to your brand.

Consistent Interaction: Regularly monitor your social media channels and make it a priority to engage with your audience. Consistent interaction helps maintain an active and engaged community.

Acknowledge Feedback: Show appreciation for both positive and negative feedback. Acknowledging constructive criticism demonstrates that you are open to improvement and value your audience's opinions.

2. Participate in Conversations:

Joining relevant discussions within your industry or community can significantly increase your visibility and credibility.

By participating in conversations, you can showcase your expertise, connect with like-minded individuals, and attract new followers.

Here are some ways to participate in conversations:

Industry Hashtags: Use popular industry-specific hashtags to join ongoing discussions and make your content discoverable to a broader audience.

Comment on Posts: Engage with posts from other industry leaders, influencers, or relevant brands. Thoughtful comments can attract attention and spark further dialogue.

Host Live Sessions: Organize live Q&A sessions, webinars, or discussions on topics of interest to your audience. Live sessions provide real-time interaction and foster a sense of community.

3. User-Generated Content:

Encouraging your followers to create content around your brand can significantly enhance engagement and build a loyal community. User-generated content (UGC) not only provides authentic social proof but also fosters a deeper connection with your audience.

Consider the following strategies for encouraging UGC:

Contests and Challenges: Launch contests or challenges that prompt your followers to create and share content related to your brand. Offer incentives, such as prizes or features on your social media channels, to encourage participation.

Feature User Content: Regularly showcase user-generated content on your social media profiles. Highlighting your followers' contributions demonstrates that you value their involvement and creativity.

Create Branded Hashtags: Develop unique, branded hashtags that your audience can use when sharing content related to your brand. Branded hashtags make it easy to track and engage with UGC.

Building a Loyal Community through Engagement:

Building a loyal community requires consistent effort and genuine interaction. By actively engaging with your audience, participating in relevant conversations, and encouraging user-generated content, you can create a vibrant and supportive community around your brand. This loyal community will not only enhance your social media presence but also contribute to the long-term success of your business.

Engaging your audience is a critical component of social media success. Active engagement, meaningful participation in conversations, and encouraging user-generated content are all effective strategies for building a loyal community.

Chapter 5: Utilizing Hashtags and SEO

Maximizing Reach

In the vast and competitive landscape of social media, effectively reaching your target audience is paramount. Leveraging hashtags and search engine optimization (SEO) strategies can significantly amplify your content's visibility and engagement.

1. Relevant Hashtags:

Hashtags are powerful tools that categorize content and make it discoverable to users interested in specific topics. Using relevant hashtags increases the likelihood of your posts being seen by your target audience. **Here's how to effectively use hashtags:**

Research Popular Hashtags: Identify the most popular and relevant hashtags in your industry. Tools like Hashtagify, RiteTag, and Instagram's search feature can help you discover trending hashtags that resonate with your audience.

Mix Popular and Niche Hashtags: While popular hashtags can increase visibility, they are also highly competitive. Incorporate a mix of popular and niche-specific hashtags to strike a balance between reach and engagement.

Create Branded Hashtags: Develop unique hashtags that reflect your brand identity. Branded hashtags encourage user-generated content and help build a community around your brand.

2. SEO Optimization:

SEO is not just for websites; it also plays a crucial role in social media. Optimizing your posts for searchability can significantly broaden your audience. **Here's how to enhance your social media SEO:**

Keyword Research: Identify relevant keywords that your target audience is searching for. Use tools like Google Keyword Planner, SEMrush, and Ahrefs to find keywords with high search volumes and low competition.

Optimize Profiles: Ensure your social media profiles are optimized with relevant keywords. Include keywords in your bio, username, and handle to improve searchability.

Use Keywords in Posts: Incorporate keywords naturally into your post captions, descriptions, and hashtags. This practice helps your content appear in search results when users look for related topics.

3. Cross-Promote Content:

Leveraging multiple platforms to cross-promote your content can exponentially increase its reach. **Here's how to effectively cross-promote:**

Share Across Platforms: Post your content on various social media platforms to reach different audience segments. Each platform has unique user demographics and engagement patterns.

Embed Social Media Links: Include links to your social media profiles on your website, email newsletters, and other digital channels to drive traffic and increase visibility.

Collaborate with Influencers: Partner with influencers and other brands to expand your reach. Influencers can introduce your content to their followers, who may become your new audience.

Maximizing Reach through Hashtags and SEO:

By strategically using relevant hashtags and optimizing your posts for SEO, you can significantly increase your content's reach and engagement. Cross-promoting your content across various platforms further amplifies your visibility, ensuring that your brand reaches a broader and more diverse audience.

Mastering the use of hashtags and SEO is essential for maximizing your reach on social media. These strategies not only enhance your content's visibility but also attract a targeted and engaged audience. By effectively utilizing hashtags, optimizing for search engines, and cross-promoting content, you can ensure that your social media presence continues to grow and thrive.

Chapter 6: Collaborations and Influencers

Expanding Your Reach

Collaborations and influencer partnerships can significantly amplify your brand's reach and credibility.

1. Strategic Partnerships:

Collaborating with influencers and other brands is a powerful way to tap into new audiences and markets. **Here's how to form effective strategic partnerships:**

Identify Relevant Influencers: Choose influencers who have a strong following within your target audience. Use tools like BuzzSumo, Klear, and HypeAuditor to find influencers whose followers align with your brand demographics.

Leverage Cross-Promotion: Partner with brands that complement your offerings. Cross-promotional campaigns allow you to introduce your brand to their audience while showcasing your partner's products or services to your followers.

Host Joint Events: Collaborate on webinars, live streams, or virtual events. Joint events not only engage your existing followers but also attract new ones from your partner's audience.

2. Authentic Collaborations:

Authenticity is key to successful collaborations.

Ensure that your partnerships resonate with your brand values and audience expectations:

Align Values and Mission: Choose collaborators whose values and mission align with yours. Authentic partnerships are more likely to generate genuine engagement and build trust with your audience.

Transparent Communication: Clearly communicate your goals and expectations with your partners. Transparency ensures that both parties are on the same page and work towards common objectives.

Create Authentic Content: Work together to create content that feels natural and authentic. Avoid overly promotional messages and focus on delivering value to your audience.

3. Mutual Benefits:

Effective collaborations should provide mutual benefits for all parties involved. **Here's how to ensure that your partnerships are mutually advantageous:**

Define Clear Goals: Establish clear goals and metrics for the collaboration. Whether it's increasing brand awareness, driving sales, or growing your follower base, having defined goals helps measure the success of the partnership.

Offer Value: Ensure that your collaboration offers value to your partner. This could be in the form of exposure to your audience, sharing resources, or providing unique content.

Evaluate and Adjust: Regularly assess the performance of your collaborations. Use analytics to measure engagement, reach, and ROI. Adjust your strategies as needed to optimize future partnerships.

Expanding Your Reach through Collaborations and Influencers:

Strategic partnerships and influencer collaborations are essential components of a comprehensive social media strategy. By identifying relevant influencers, forming authentic collaborations, and ensuring mutual benefits, you can significantly expand your reach and enhance your brand's credibility.

Collaborations and influencer partnerships offer a powerful way to amplify your social media presence. By strategically selecting partners, aligning values, and creating mutually beneficial relationships, you can reach new audiences and build a stronger, more engaged community around your brand.

Chapter 7: Consistency is Key

Building Momentum

Consistency is a crucial element in building and maintaining a strong social media presence. It ensures that your audience knows when to expect new content, which helps in keeping them engaged and coming back for more.

1. Regular Posting:

Maintaining a consistent posting schedule is vital for several reasons:

Audience Expectation: Regular posting sets expectations for your audience. When followers know they can rely on you for fresh content at specific times, they are more likely to stay engaged and look forward to your posts.

Algorithm Favorability: Social media algorithms favor accounts that post consistently. Regular activity signals to platforms that your account is active and relevant, which can improve your content's visibility.

Building Habit: Just as you want your followers to form a habit of engaging with your content, you should also establish a routine for creating and posting content. This habit helps in maintaining a steady flow of content and prevents burnout.

2. Content Calendar:

Planning your posts in advance using a content calendar is an effective way to ensure regularity:

Organized Planning: A content calendar helps you organize your posting schedule, plan for upcoming events, and ensure a balanced mix of content types (e.g., promotional, educational, entertaining).

Time Management: By planning ahead, you can allocate time for content creation, editing, and scheduling, which reduces the last-minute rush and stress.

Consistency: A content calendar ensures that there are no gaps in your posting schedule, maintaining a consistent presence on social media. It also allows you to coordinate posts across different platforms, ensuring a cohesive strategy.

3. Adapting Strategies:

Regularly assessing and adapting your strategies based on performance metrics is essential for sustained success:

Performance Metrics: Use analytics tools to monitor the performance of your posts. Metrics such as engagement rates, reach, and conversion rates provide insights into what is working and what isn't.

Feedback Loop: Use the data collected from performance metrics to create a feedback loop. Identify trends, understand your audience's preferences, and adjust your content strategy accordingly.

Flexibility: Be open to changing your strategies based on the feedback you receive. Social media trends and audience preferences can change rapidly, so staying flexible and adaptive is key to maintaining relevance.

Building Momentum through Consistency:

Consistency in posting builds momentum and helps in establishing a strong connection with your audience. It not only enhances your visibility but also builds trust and reliability.

When your audience knows they can depend on you for regular, high-quality content, they are more likely to remain loyal and engaged.

Consistency is the cornerstone of a successful social media strategy. By maintaining a regular posting schedule, utilizing a content calendar, and adapting your strategies based on performance metrics, you can build and sustain momentum.

Chapter 8: Real-Life Success Stories

Case Study: Sourceless Inc.

Sourceless Inc. is a prime example of how cutting-edge technology and sophisticated marketing strategies can drive substantial growth. Under my guidance, Sourceless Inc. leveraged blockchain innovations to carve a niche in a competitive market. We employed advanced SEO techniques, targeted content marketing, and strategic social media campaigns to enhance user engagement. These efforts resulted in significant market penetration, demonstrating the power of a well-executed digital marketing strategy. The integration of organic growth tactics ensured sustained visibility and user retention, highlighting the effectiveness of a holistic approach to digital marketing.

Case Study: AI Marketing and Bumble Vector

AI Marketing and Bumble Vector illustrate the transformative impact of comprehensive digital marketing campaigns. These companies faced the challenge of boosting client visibility and increasing customer acquisition rates in a crowded digital space. Our strategy began with in-depth market research to identify target demographics and key engagement channels.

SEO Optimization: We optimized their websites and content for search engines, improving their organic search rankings and driving high-quality traffic.

Social Media Management: We created and managed dynamic social media profiles, posting regular, engaging content that resonated with their audience.

Content Marketing: High-quality, informative content was developed to position these companies as thought leaders in their fields. Blog posts, articles, and multimedia content were crafted to provide value to their audience and encourage sharing.

Analytics and Adjustments: Continuous monitoring of campaign performance allowed us to make data-driven adjustments, ensuring maximum effectiveness.

The results were remarkable. Both AI Marketing and Bumble Vector experienced a surge in website traffic, higher engagement rates on social media, and a significant increase in customer acquisition.

The integration of SEO, social media management, and content marketing created a cohesive and impactful online presence. This holistic approach not only attracted new customers but also fostered a loyal community around their brands.

These case studies exemplify the potential of strategic digital marketing in achieving business growth. By focusing on organic growth and leveraging advanced marketing techniques, we can create sustainable success and establish a strong online presence.

Chapter 9: My Methodology

In-Depth Analysis and Customized Strategies

My methodology starts with a comprehensive analysis of each client's unique needs and market position.

This step involves understanding their business goals, target audience, competitive landscape, and current digital presence.

By gathering this information, I can identify strengths, weaknesses, opportunities, and threats (SWOT analysis) that shape the strategic direction.

Once the analysis is complete, I craft customized strategies tailored to leverage the latest digital marketing tools and techniques.

This includes SEO optimization, content marketing, social media management, and more.

Each strategy is designed to align with the client's business goals, ensuring that every action taken contributes to their overarching objectives.

In-Depth Analysis

The initial phase involves several key components:

Market Research: Understanding industry trends, competitor strategies, and consumer behavior to identify opportunities for differentiation.

Audience Profiling: Creating detailed profiles of the target audience to tailor content and engagement strategies effectively.

SWOT Analysis: Evaluating the strengths, weaknesses, opportunities, and threats to craft a strategic plan that leverages strengths and addresses weaknesses.

Customized Strategies

Once the analysis is complete, I develop bespoke strategies that utilize the latest digital marketing tools and techniques. **These strategies are multi-faceted and integrated, encompassing:**

SEO Optimization: Improving search engine rankings to drive organic traffic. This involves keyword research, on-page optimization, and link-building strategies.

Content Marketing: Creating valuable, engaging content that resonates with the target audience. This includes blog posts, articles, videos, infographics, and more.

Social Media Management: Developing and managing social media profiles to engage with the audience, build brand loyalty, and drive traffic to the website.

Email Marketing: Crafting targeted email campaigns to nurture leads and convert them into customers.

Analytics and Reporting: Continuously monitoring performance metrics to assess the effectiveness of strategies and make data-driven adjustments.

Regular Progress Assessments

To ensure that the strategies remain aligned with business goals, I conduct regular progress assessments. **These assessments involve:**

Performance Metrics: Tracking key performance indicators (KPIs) such as website traffic, conversion rates, social media engagement, and more.

Feedback Loop: Gathering feedback from the client and their customers to understand what's working and what needs improvement.

Strategy Adjustments: Making necessary adjustments to strategies based on performance data and feedback to maximize effectiveness and achieve desired outcomes.

Adapting to Change

In the ever-evolving digital landscape, staying adaptable is crucial. **My methodology includes:**

Continuous Learning: Keeping abreast of the latest trends, tools, and technologies in digital marketing to incorporate into strategies.

Flexibility: Being prepared to pivot strategies quickly in response to market changes, new opportunities, or unforeseen challenges.

Innovation: Experimenting with new approaches and creative solutions to stay ahead of the competition and continually deliver exceptional results for clients.

Chapter 10: The First Step

Starting Your Journey

Embarking on the journey to build a robust social media presence can be daunting, but together, we'll navigate this path to success. With nearly two decades of experience in digital marketing and business development, I bring a wealth of knowledge and innovative strategies to the table.

Over the years, I've had the privilege of collaborating with technology companies across the United States, the UK, Germany, Romania, and Italy, as well as numerous NGOs. These diverse experiences have equipped me with a comprehensive understanding of various markets and audience dynamics. My work has included the creation of hundreds of websites, the design of thousands of vectors, and the rigorous testing of numerous marketing platforms.

The key to my approach lies in the balance between creativity and data-driven strategies. This blend ensures that your brand's growth is not only rapid but also sustainable. By focusing on organic growth, we lay a solid foundation that supports long-term success.

Your Personalized Roadmap

Our journey begins with a detailed understanding of your business. We'll delve into your goals, target audience, and competitive landscape. This initial phase is crucial as it shapes the strategies we develop.

Brand Discovery: We'll explore the essence of your brand, identifying what makes it unique and how it resonates with your audience.

Goal Setting: Defining clear, measurable goals that align with your business objectives. These goals will guide our strategy and provide benchmarks for success.

Strategic Implementation

With a solid understanding of your brand and goals, we move to the strategic phase. Here, we craft a bespoke plan tailored to your unique needs.

SEO and Content Strategy: Implementing robust SEO practices to enhance your search engine visibility. Creating high-quality, valuable content that speaks directly to your audience.

Social Media Management: Developing a cohesive social media strategy that includes regular posting schedules, engaging content, and active interaction with followers.

Performance Monitoring: Regularly assessing the performance of our strategies through detailed analytics and feedback loops. This allows us to make necessary adjustments and stay aligned with your goals.

Collaboration and Support

Throughout this process, you'll have a dedicated partner committed to your success. We believe in transparent communication and collaborative effort.

Regular Updates: Keeping you informed about progress with detailed reports and insights.

Open Communication: Ensuring that you're always in the loop and have a clear understanding of our strategies and their impact.

Adaptability: Staying flexible and ready to pivot strategies in response to new opportunities or challenges.

Experience and Expertise

My extensive experience spans various sectors and geographies, providing a broad perspective on digital marketing and business growth. From working with tech giants to supporting NGOs, each project has contributed to a deep well of knowledge that I bring to every new client.

Taking the First Step Together

The first step is indeed the hardest, but it's also the most crucial. It sets the tone for your journey and establishes the foundation for future growth. With my guidance, you won't take this step alone. We'll work together to ensure that your brand not only achieves its initial goals but continues to thrive in the competitive digital landscape.

By combining innovative strategies with tried-and-tested methods, we will navigate the complexities of digital marketing, build a loyal and engaged follower base, and drive sustainable growth for your brand. This book serves as your guide, offering insights and practical advice to help you succeed.

Conclusion: Embracing Organic Growth for Long-Term Success

Organic growth is the cornerstone of building a strong, sustainable online presence. This book has walked you through the critical steps to achieve this, from understanding the importance of the first 1,000 followers to crafting quality content, engaging your audience, and leveraging SEO and strategic partnerships.

For businesses ready to elevate their digital journey, I offer a proven path to success. My unique combination of organic growth strategies ensures that companies build a strong, engaged follower base, paving the way for long-term success in the digital landscape.

By focusing on authentic engagement and high-quality content, you can create a loyal community that not only supports your brand but also advocates for it. The first 1,000 followers are the bedrock upon which your online success is built. Their genuine interest and engagement provide valuable feedback, enhance your visibility through favorable algorithms, and establish trust and credibility.

As we explored in the case studies of Sourceless Inc., AI Marketing, and Bumble Vector, a strategic approach to digital marketing can lead to remarkable growth and market penetration. These successes underscore the power of integrating SEO, social media management, and content marketing into a cohesive strategy.

My methodology, involving in-depth analysis and customized strategies, ensures that every action taken aligns with your business goals. Regular progress assessments and adaptability to new opportunities or challenges keep the strategies effective and relevant.

Embarking on this journey might seem daunting, but with nearly two decades of experience in digital marketing and business development, I am here to guide you. Over the years, I have collaborated with technology companies in the United States, the UK, Germany, Romania, Italy, and numerous NGOs, creating a solid foundation of knowledge and innovative approaches.

Let's take the first step together and transform your business's social media presence. Contact me through www.iulianbondari.com to discover how my expertise can help you achieve lasting success in the digital space.

Building a strong social media presence starts with organic growth. By focusing on authenticity, engagement, and high-quality content, you lay the groundwork for sustainable success. This book is your guide to navigating the complexities of digital marketing and achieving your business goals.

Together, we'll create a robust online presence that stands the test of time.